"Dyeing" to Win

by Kristi McGee
illustrated by Deborah White

HARCOURT
SCHOOL PUBLISHERS

D1784177

Printed in China

ISBN 10:   0-15-377417-7
ISBN 13:   978-0-15-377417-1

Ordering Options
ISBN 10:   0-15-377149-6 (Grade 5 Collection)
ISBN 13:   978-0-15-377149-1 (Grade 5 Collection)
ISBN 10:   0-15-377875-X (package of 5)
ISBN 13:   978-0-15-377875-9 (package of 5)

2 3 4 5 6 7 8 9 10   0940   17 16 15 14 13 12 11 10 09

Let's get one thing clear. I am a winner. I always have been. I have a downright phobia of losing. I am the fastest runner on the block. When I was in kindergarten, Johnny Epstein challenged me to see who could run faster. To my horror, he won. After that day, I promised myself I wouldn't lose again. Every day after school, I practiced running. I got really good. I learned that to be the best at anything, you had to practice every day, so I did.

I am also the best speller in my class. No one can spell words better than I can. I won the fourth grade spelling bee last year. I had to spell *copacetic* for the win. That means "everything is okay." It was—because I won. I am also the best at math in my class, and science. Don't get me wrong. It is hard to be the best at everything. It means I am not only a winner; I am also a loner.

Once a year I feel like the most popular kid in class. That is during science fair time. Everyone wants to be my partner. They know that with me, they will win. They also know they won't have to do much work.

This year is going to be different, though. I am going to ask Jacob to be my partner. He is the second smartest kid in the class. Everyone wants to be his partner, too. I think if the two of us work on the project together, it will be a guaranteed win. Neither of us will have to do all the work. It is a win-win situation—just what I like.

This morning Mrs. O'Hurley announced the science fair dates. At recess I immediately went up to Jacob and told him my plan. He agreed. He knows what it is like to have to do all the work. He has done it every year, too. Even though all the kids in the class asked both of us to be their partners, we were not swayed. We can sympathize with each other. Now we need to find a winning idea for a project.

Mrs. O'Hurley gave us time to work with our partners. We were to come up with ideas for a project. Jacob said we should do something with the stars. We couldn't think of any questions to ask, though. Also, it is hard to see any stars here. The bright lights of the big city wash them out.

We wanted something that had an awesome delivery. We wanted to make an impression. I suggested we make a volcano. We could measure lava flow. It was a great idea! When we did a little research, we saw it would be way too expensive. We would have to buy a model volcano and a three-dimensional map to start. We vetoed that idea.

We needed something that would wow the audience. It needed to be inexpensive and practical for our resources. Finally, we came up with the answer. We would test fruits, vegetables and plants to see which one made the best dye. We didn't need much, just a few vegetables, a big pot, and something to dye. We could manage that!

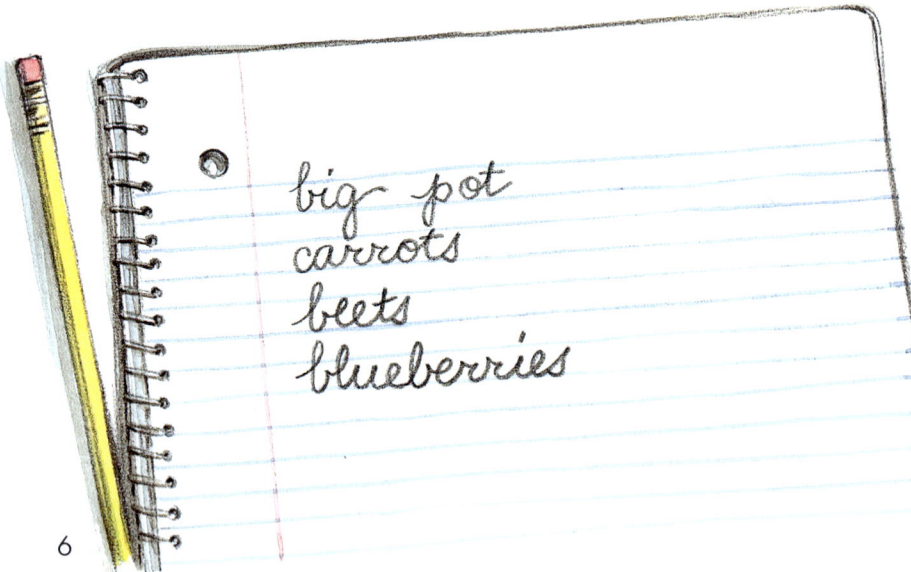

big pot
carrots
beets
blueberries

I told my mom about the project that night. I called Jacob, and we planned a trip to the grocery store and the fabric store. We picked up carrots, lettuce, celery, blueberries, and beets. We also got a bunch of white cotton fabric on sale. After our shopping trip, Jacob came over. We cut the white cotton fabric into small squares to use to test whether the dye would work. Then we decided we'd done enough for one day. It was late.

The next week we spent on research. I was in charge
of making the dye, not that Jacob didn't help. He was in
charge of dyeing the fabric. I figured out what to mix with
the vegetables to make specific colors. I also learned how
long they had to cook and at what temperature.

On Saturday, Jacob came over again. We decided to
start with the carrots. Our first attempt to make a dye was
a bust. The carrots didn't really color anything. We were
rather disappointed. At least we got some pictures of the
process, and we knew what didn't work.

The next weekend we moved onto the lettuce and celery. Those were no good either. The blueberries and beets were great, though. They turned the fabric a pretty blue and a bright pinkish red. We had found two winners. The beets were the most striking of the two.

Now we had to find one more plant to use as a dye. We sat on the front stoop to think. I looked over at the trellis by our porch. The bright green leaves of the clematis plant spoke to me. I asked my mom before I picked a few. She said it needed to be trimmed anyway. We took the leaves upstairs, and—abracadabra!—we had yellow dye after a few hours of brewing.

The science fair was fast approaching. Jacob and I decided we needed to dye something more fun than just a piece of cloth. "Maybe," Jacob suggested, "we could dye something people could wear."

I thought that was a great idea. He decided to donate a white shirt. I thought it would look nice if it were blue. I couldn't find anything white in my closet that I wanted to color. Jacob suggested my white stuffed bear. I hesitated at first, but I thought he might look cute in yellow. Jacob said he would take care of dyeing something bright red. He claimed he had a great idea as to what he would dye red. However, he wouldn't tell me what it was.

He said, "Don't worry, you'll see at the fair."

By the end of the week, we had all our posters together. On fair day, I was really excited. We had worked really hard on our project. Jacob showed up on time. It was warm, but he was wearing a winter hat. He said he had overslept and that his hair was a mess. I certainly knew what that was like. We quickly got to business setting up our display.

We hung our sign that read, WHICH PLANTS DYE BEST? We had pictures of the dyeing process. Some were pretty funny, though mom didn't really think so. Her whole kitchen looked blue at one point. She called it the blueberry invasion. We displayed each of the items we had used to make the dye in its own compartment in a box. We put the fabric pieces with no results from the carrots, lettuce, and celery under their pictures. Then we set up the top three contenders: clematis leaves, blueberries, and beets. Finally, we set out the items we had dyed. My bear looked adorable. It had yellow wispy fur. It had turned out really well. Jacob's newly "blueberry" shirt was perfect. The color was evenly placed. Our presentation looked pretty good, but something was missing.

I was dying of curiosity, no pun intended, to find out what Jacob had dyed red. Jacob didn't have anything with him that was beet-red. I asked him again what it was that he had dyed. He assured me that I would find out soon enough. When the judges came to our booth, Jacob still hadn't produced a beet-red anything. My stomach was in my throat, and my heart was in my stomach. I was so nervous. Like I said, I have a phobia of losing.

The judges looked through our posters, our pictures, and our notes on the process. Then one of the judges noticed that we were missing a red item. "How come there is nothing here where the red item should be?" he asked.

That's when Jacob worked his magic.

"Can I have your attention, please?" Jacob said to the judges. He certainly had mine. They all turned and looked at him.

"For the first-place winner of the best vegetable dye, I give you the beet!" Jacob announced as he ripped his hat off his head.

His pale blond hair was gone. It was replaced with beet-red hair! All the judges burst into laughter—so did I. I knew at that moment, we had won the contest.

Think Critically

1. What is the main idea of the story?

2. What details does the narrator use to support the main idea?

3. From what point of view is the story told?

4. How do you feel about winning? How do your feelings compare to the ideas presented in the story?

5. Why is the narrator surprised at the end of the story? Were you? Explain why or why not?

 **Science**

Your Own Science Project Come up with an idea for your own science fair project. Phrase the idea as a question you want to answer with an experiment. Then write a plan to complete the project. What supplies will you need? What do you need to do to complete the project?

School-Home Connection Tell a family member about this story. Then share your ideas for a science fair project with him or her.

Word Count: 1,402